Screen Scripts

Creative writing activities using multi-media

Authors: Blair Bielawski
        Emily Streckert
Editorial Assistance: Elizabeth Jorgensen
Cover and Book Design: Patti Jeffers

Printed in the United States of America

ISBN 978-1-4291-0395-4

BRIDGING
the Gaps in Education™
Lorenz Educational Press
P.O. Box 802 • Dayton, OH 45401
www.LorenzEducationalPress.com

The activities in *Screen Scripts* support the following standards recommended by the National Council of Teachers of English and the International Reading Association:

4. Students adjust their use of spoken, written, and visual language (e.g., conventions, style, vocabulary) to communicate effectively with a variety of audiences and for different purposes.

5. Students employ a wide range of strategies as they write and use different writing process elements appropriately to communicate with different audiences for a variety of purposes.

6. Students apply knowledge of language structure, language conventions (e.g., spelling and punctuation), media techniques, figurative language, and genre to create, critique, and discuss print and non-print texts.

7. Students conduct research on issues and interests by generating ideas and questions, and by posing problems. They gather, evaluate, and synthesize data from a variety of sources (e.g., print and non-print texts, artifacts, people) to communicate their discoveries in ways that suit their purpose and audience.

8. Students use a variety of technological and information resources (e.g., libraries, databases, computer networks, video) to gather and synthesize information and to create and communicate knowledge.

12. Students use spoken, written, and visual language to accomplish their own purposes (e.g., for learning, enjoyment, persuasion, and the exchange of information).

Supports

NCTE and IRA Standards

Table of Contents

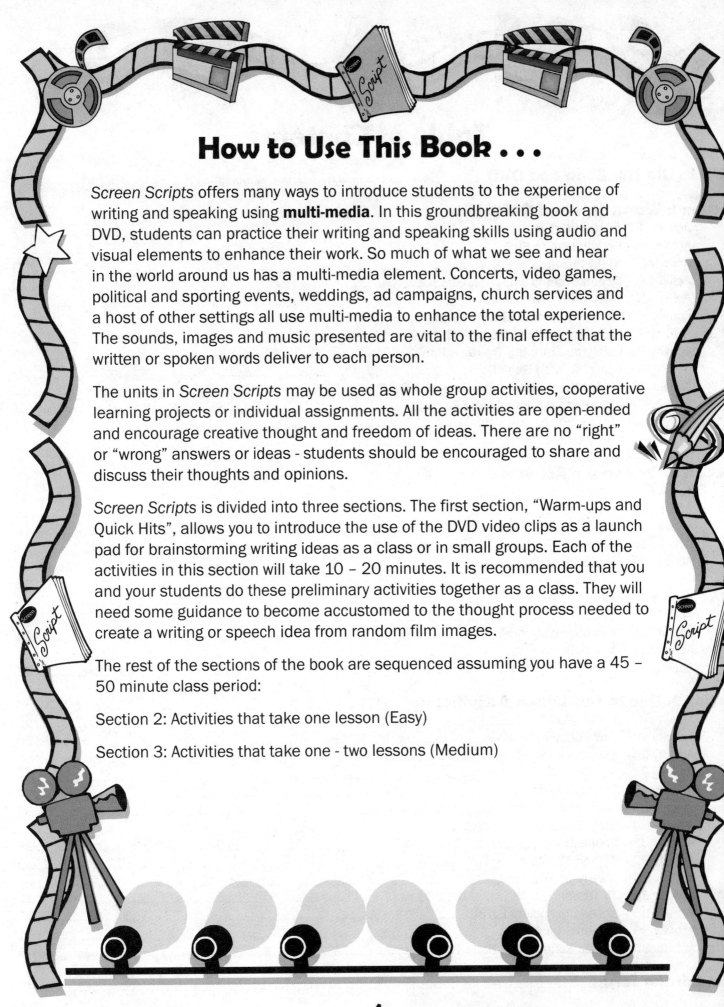

How to Use This Book . . .

Screen Scripts offers many ways to introduce students to the experience of writing and speaking using **multi-media**. In this groundbreaking book and DVD, students can practice their writing and speaking skills using audio and visual elements to enhance their work. So much of what we see and hear in the world around us has a multi-media element. Concerts, video games, political and sporting events, weddings, ad campaigns, church services and a host of other settings all use multi-media to enhance the total experience. The sounds, images and music presented are vital to the final effect that the written or spoken words deliver to each person.

The units in *Screen Scripts* may be used as whole group activities, cooperative learning projects or individual assignments. All the activities are open-ended and encourage creative thought and freedom of ideas. There are no "right" or "wrong" answers or ideas - students should be encouraged to share and discuss their thoughts and opinions.

Screen Scripts is divided into three sections. The first section, "Warm-ups and Quick Hits", allows you to introduce the use of the DVD video clips as a launch pad for brainstorming writing ideas as a class or in small groups. Each of the activities in this section will take 10 – 20 minutes. It is recommended that you and your students do these preliminary activities together as a class. They will need some guidance to become accustomed to the thought process needed to create a writing or speech idea from random film images.

The rest of the sections of the book are sequenced assuming you have a 45 – 50 minute class period:

Section 2: Activities that take one lesson (Easy)

Section 3: Activities that take one - two lessons (Medium)

How to Use the DVD . . .

he included DVD will play in any standard DVD player and may also be played using a computer loaded
ith the software necessary to read a DVD. Use the remote just as you would with any standard DVD
 scroll through the different film groups. The arrows on each screen move you between menu pages.
ighlight a title and press 'enter' to view a particular clip.

here are ten film "banks" on the DVD. Each of these banks includes a 30 – 45 second film clip that
 presented four times. The first time the clip is shown with no background music. The next three clips
resent the same scene with radically different styles of music in the background. The ten film banks are:

1. Ancient Egypt
2. Crystal Effects
3. Do You Like to Fly?
4. From the Treetops
5. Night Vision
6. Mad Rush
7. March of the Penguins
8. Ocean's Island
9. Tales of the Tribesmen
10. Episode in Space

each of these ten banks, the clips are numbered 1 – 4, and the first clip is always the one with no
usic.

addition, there are three bonus video banks...five videos for the "News Break" activity perfect for use
 a current events unit (found on page 17), five videos for the "Now Sell It" activity (page 33) and five
deos for the longer activities in Section 3 of the book.

u can begin by simply having your students create titles for some of the film clips included on the
/D. Other ideas and resources included in the book will help you create sequenced lessons that will
ide your students through the creative process. You will almost certainly find dozens of ways to use
e DVD beyond what we have designed in the accompanying book. Some other possible applications
clude:

1. Independent Study
2. Enrichment/Extension
3. Speech Presentation
4. Team Building

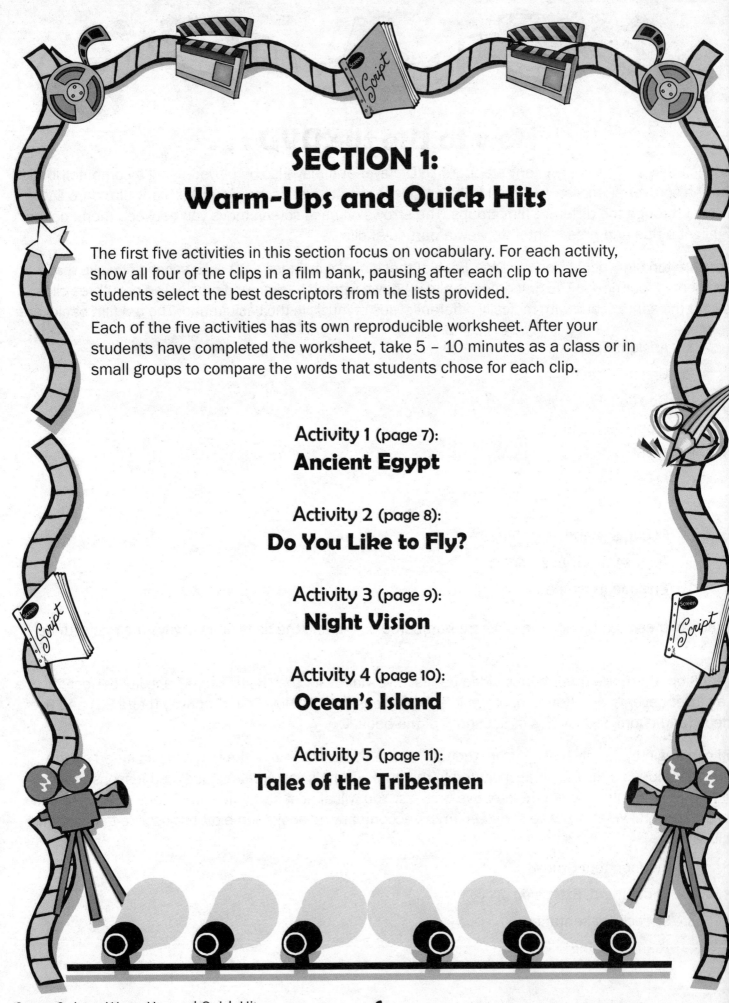

SECTION 1:
Warm-Ups and Quick Hits

The first five activities in this section focus on vocabulary. For each activity, show all four of the clips in a film bank, pausing after each clip to have students select the best descriptors from the lists provided.

Each of the five activities has its own reproducible worksheet. After your students have completed the worksheet, take 5 – 10 minutes as a class or in small groups to compare the words that students chose for each clip.

ame _____ Date_____

Ancient Egypt

You will see a short film clip four times. There will be a pause after each clip.
Put an "X" next to the words that you think best describe each clip.

Clip #1	Clip #2
_____ exciting	_____ carefree
_____ slow	_____ dull
_____ adventurous	_____ joyful
_____ fast	_____ scary
_____ dangerous	_____ festive
_____ boring	_____ hazardous
_____ delightful	_____ bright
_____ mysterious	_____ slow
_____ comical	_____ sad
_____ jovial	_____ anticipation

Clip #3	Clip #4
_____ mysterious	_____ bizarre
_____ scary	_____ shadowy
_____ delightful	_____ joyful
_____ exciting	_____ mystical
_____ boring	_____ dangerous
_____ fast	_____ slow
_____ boisterous	_____ dull
_____ magical	_____ frightful
_____ fun	_____ gloomy
_____ carefree	_____ outrageous

Name _____   Date _____

Do You Like to Fly?

You will see a short film clip four times. There will be a pause after each clip.
Put an "X" next to the words that you think best describe each clip.

Clip #1	Clip #2
_____ exciting	_____ carefree
_____ slow	_____ tranquil
_____ adventurous	_____ joyful
_____ fast	_____ scary
_____ dangerous	_____ festive
_____ boring	_____ hazardous
_____ delightful	_____ bright
_____ mysterious	_____ slow
_____ sad	_____ sad
_____ jovial	_____ fun

Clip #3	Clip #4
_____ mysterious	_____ cheerful
_____ scary	_____ shadowy
_____ boisterous	_____ joyful
_____ exciting	_____ mystical
_____ boring	_____ bizarre
_____ fast	_____ slow
_____ believable	_____ dull
_____ magical	_____ frightful
_____ fun	_____ gloomy
_____ carefree	_____ exciting

ame _____   Date_____

Night Vision

You will see a short film clip four times. There will be a pause after each clip.
Put an "X" next to the words that you think best describe each clip.

Clip #1	Clip #2
_____ exciting	_____ carefree
_____ slow	_____ dull
_____ adventurous	_____ joyful
_____ fast	_____ scary
_____ outrageous	_____ festive
_____ boring	_____ hazardous
_____ delightful	_____ bright
_____ mysterious	_____ slow
_____ comical	_____ sad
_____ happy	_____ fun

Clip #3	Clip #4
_____ mysterious	_____ cheerful
_____ scary	_____ shadowy
_____ delightful	_____ joyful
_____ exciting	_____ mystical
_____ boring	_____ dangerous
_____ fast	_____ slow
_____ believable	_____ dull
_____ magical	_____ frightful
_____ fun	_____ gloomy
_____ carefree	_____ exciting

Ocean's Island

You will see a short film clip four times. There will be a pause after each clip.
Put an "X" next to the words that you think best describe each clip.

Clip #1	Clip #2
_____ tranquil	_____ carefree
_____ slow	_____ dull
_____ adventurous	_____ joyful
_____ fast	_____ scary
_____ dangerous	_____ festive
_____ boring	_____ emotional
_____ delightful	_____ comical
_____ mysterious	_____ slow
_____ gloomy	_____ sad
_____ happy	_____ fun

Clip #3	Clip #4
_____ mysterious	_____ cheerful
_____ scary	_____ shadowy
_____ delightful	_____ joyful
_____ exciting	_____ mystical
_____ boring	_____ boisterous
_____ fast	_____ slow
_____ believable	_____ dull
_____ magical	_____ frightful
_____ fun	_____ gloomy
_____ carefree	_____ exciting

Name _____   Date_____

Tales of the Tribesmen

You will see a short film clip four times. There will be a pause after each clip.
Put an "X" next to the words that you think best describe each clip.

Clip #1	Clip #2
_____ exciting	_____ jovial
_____ slow	_____ dull
_____ adventurous	_____ joyful
_____ fast	_____ scary
_____ dangerous	_____ festive
_____ boring	_____ hazardous
_____ delightful	_____ bright
_____ mysterious	_____ slow
_____ emotional	_____ sad
_____ happy	_____ fun

Clip #3	Clip #4
_____ mysterious	_____ cheerful
_____ scary	_____ shadowy
_____ delightful	_____ joyful
_____ exciting	_____ mystical
_____ boring	_____ dangerous
_____ fast	_____ slow
_____ believable	_____ dull
_____ magical	_____ frightful
_____ fun	_____ gloomy
_____ carefree	_____ exciting

Activity 6
Using the **Crystal Effects** Bank

Play Clips #2, 3 and 4 from this bank. Pause after each one and have students imagine what kind of television show might use that clip. Here are some ideas to help get them started...

1. Documentary
2. Science Fiction
3. Action/Adventure
4. Police Stories
5. Sports
6. Drama

7. Comedy
8. Animated/Cartoon
9. Reality
10. News
11. Game show
12. "Do it Yourself"

After you have reviewed the clips as a class, have the students write a paragraph that begins:
"I think Clip #_____ is from a _____ because..."

You may wish to create a card for each category and have the students vote. Allow discussion to suppo point of view. This can be an excellent lead-in to purposeful persuasive writing to convince a group to "feel" a particular clip in the "same" way.

Activity 7
Using the **Do You Like to Fly?** Bank

Play Clip #1 from this bank. Based on the topography, where do your students think this might have been filmed? How many descriptive words or phrases can they think of that would help a reader imagine this scene? List the words on the board, or have the students write down five (or more) words and share them in small groups.

Activity 8
Using the **From the Treetops** Bank

Play Clip #3 from this bank. Write down words and phrases on the board that your students suggest to describe how they think the monkey feels. Next, play Clip #4 from the same bank. Does the different music in this clip suggest different feelings the monkey might have? Do the students think that the same list of words would work for both Clip #3 and Clip #4?

Have your students write a paragraph that describes either Clip #3 or #4 using some or all of the word that the class suggested.

Activity 9
Using the **Mad Rush** Bank

Play Clip #1 from this bank. What kinds of feelings do your students think people have when they are in large crowds? in big cities? in traffic jams? What feelings do they have themselves? Have the students write a paragraph describing a time they were in a crowd. Be sure to have them include some sensory details!

Activity 10
Using the **March of the Penguins** Bank

Play Clip #1 from this bank. On the board, write down students' ideas about the pros and cons of being a penguin. Individually or in small groups, have the students develop a topic sentence for a paragraph about the *positive aspects* of being a penguin. Then, have them create a topic sentence for a paragraph about the *negative aspects* of a penguin's life. Let them choose a position (pro or con) and write a paragraph using one of the topic sentences they have already created.

Activity 11
Using the **Ocean's Island** Bank

Play Clip #1 from this bank. Have your students imagine that they are being transported to this remote, uninhabited island, and they will be there for a year. What are five things they would definitely want to bring with them? What are things they would miss the most? Have them write down their lists and share them with the class.

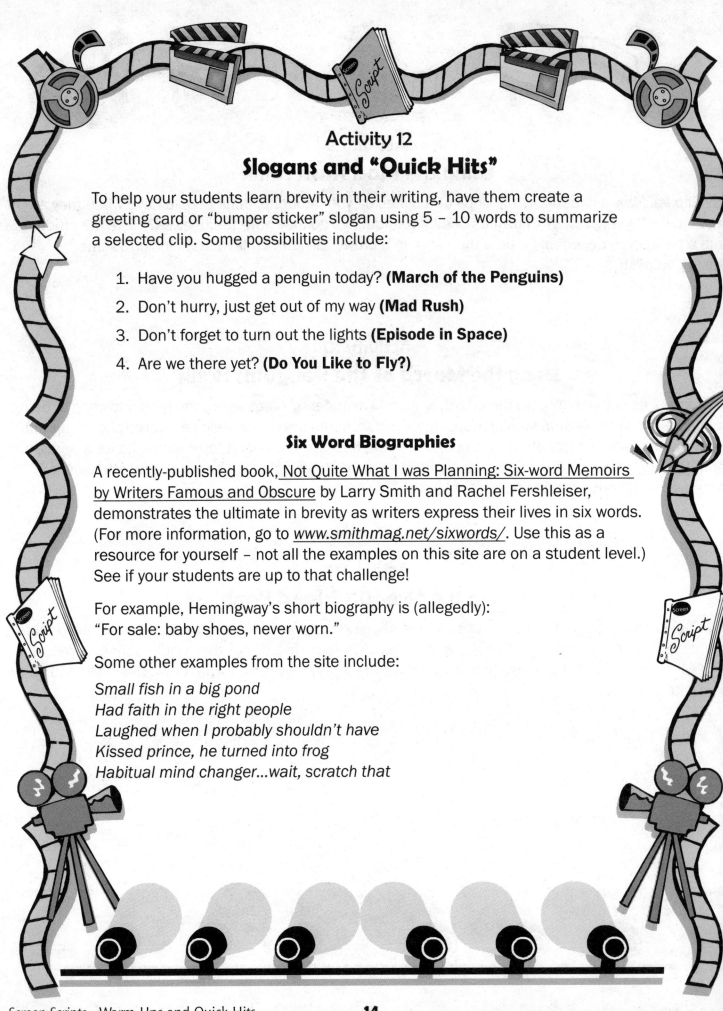

Activity 12
Slogans and "Quick Hits"

To help your students learn brevity in their writing, have them create a greeting card or "bumper sticker" slogan using 5 – 10 words to summarize a selected clip. Some possibilities include:

1. Have you hugged a penguin today? **(March of the Penguins)**

2. Don't hurry, just get out of my way **(Mad Rush)**

3. Don't forget to turn out the lights **(Episode in Space)**

4. Are we there yet? **(Do You Like to Fly?)**

Six Word Biographies

A recently-published book, Not Quite What I was Planning: Six-word Memoirs by Writers Famous and Obscure by Larry Smith and Rachel Fershleiser, demonstrates the ultimate in brevity as writers express their lives in six words. (For more information, go to *www.smithmag.net/sixwords/*. Use this as a resource for yourself – not all the examples on this site are on a student level.) See if your students are up to that challenge!

For example, Hemingway's short biography is (allegedly):
"For sale: baby shoes, never worn."

Some other examples from the site include:

Small fish in a big pond
Had faith in the right people
Laughed when I probably shouldn't have
Kissed prince, he turned into frog
Habitual mind changer...wait, scratch that

SECTION 2:
One Lesson Activities
(Based on a 45 – 50 minute class period)

Activity 13
What's in a Name?

The purpose of this activity is to help get your students involved in the creative process by inventing titles for several of the film clips included on the DVD. There are ten different film clip banks, and each bank contains a film clip that is presented four times. Select any of the film clip banks below and then show your class the first clip in the set – the one with no music.

1. **Ancient Egypt**

2. **Crystal Effects**

3. **Do You Like to Fly?**

4. **From the Treetops**

5. **Night Vision**

6. **Mad Rush**

7. **March of the Penguins**

8. **Ocean's Island**

9. **Tales of the Tribesmen**

10. **Episode in Space**

Next, discuss the clip with your class. What was the overall mood? Where might the clip have been filmed? How did the scenery look? What was the pace of the clip? After the discussion, have the students agree on a title for the clip.

Now, show the first clip with music. Discuss the clip again focusing on how the music affected the movie clip. Did it make it funny, scary, dramatic, romantic, cute, or suspenseful? How did it change the student's perceptions from the clip with no music? See if the class can come up with a different title for this clip. Repeat this activity with the remaining two clips in the bank. You may then select a different bank and go through the process again with the entire class, or have a small group work together to create titles for a different bank.

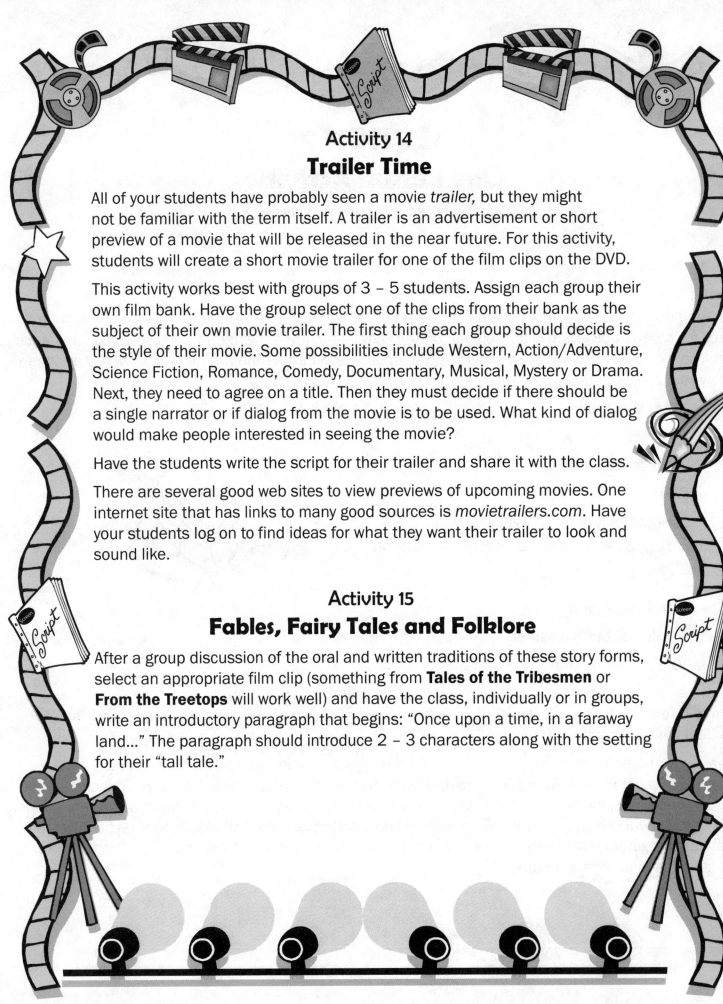

Activity 14

Trailer Time

All of your students have probably seen a movie *trailer,* but they might not be familiar with the term itself. A trailer is an advertisement or short preview of a movie that will be released in the near future. For this activity, students will create a short movie trailer for one of the film clips on the DVD.

This activity works best with groups of 3 – 5 students. Assign each group their own film bank. Have the group select one of the clips from their bank as the subject of their own movie trailer. The first thing each group should decide is the style of their movie. Some possibilities include Western, Action/Adventure, Science Fiction, Romance, Comedy, Documentary, Musical, Mystery or Drama. Next, they need to agree on a title. Then they must decide if there should be a single narrator or if dialog from the movie is to be used. What kind of dialog would make people interested in seeing the movie?

Have the students write the script for their trailer and share it with the class.

There are several good web sites to view previews of upcoming movies. One internet site that has links to many good sources is *movietrailers.com.* Have your students log on to find ideas for what they want their trailer to look and sound like.

Activity 15

Fables, Fairy Tales and Folklore

After a group discussion of the oral and written traditions of these story forms, select an appropriate film clip (something from **Tales of the Tribesmen** or **From the Treetops** will work well) and have the class, individually or in groups, write an introductory paragraph that begins: "Once upon a time, in a faraway land..." The paragraph should introduce 2 – 3 characters along with the setting for their "tall tale."

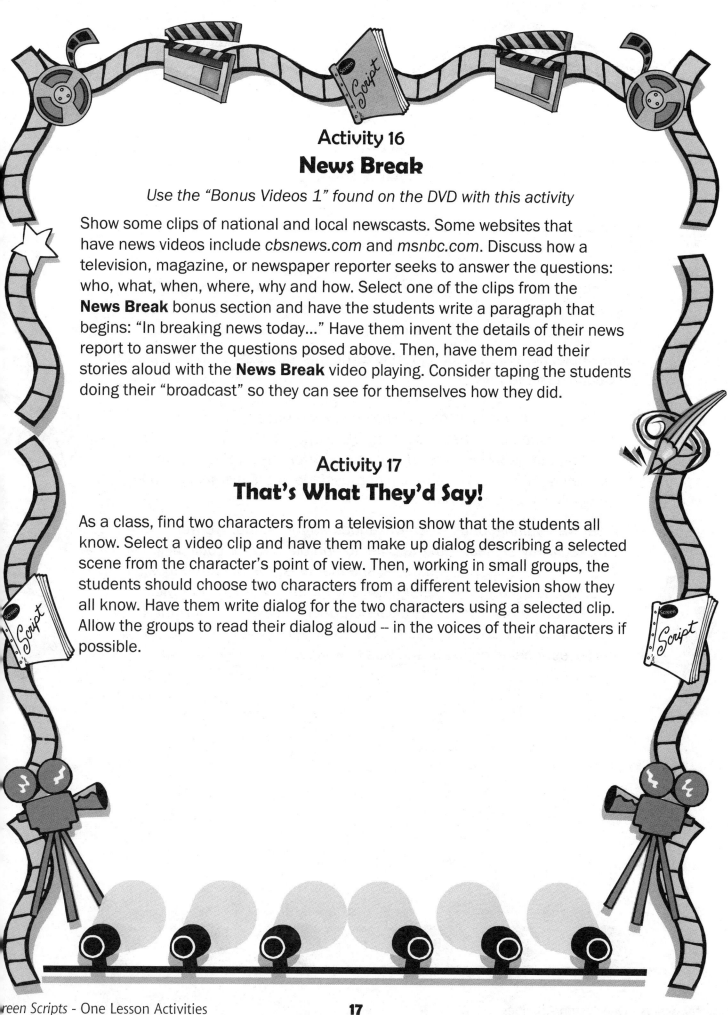

Activity 16
News Break

Use the "Bonus Videos 1" found on the DVD with this activity

Show some clips of national and local newscasts. Some websites that have news videos include *cbsnews.com* and *msnbc.com*. Discuss how a television, magazine, or newspaper reporter seeks to answer the questions: who, what, when, where, why and how. Select one of the clips from the **News Break** bonus section and have the students write a paragraph that begins: "In breaking news today..." Have them invent the details of their news report to answer the questions posed above. Then, have them read their stories aloud with the **News Break** video playing. Consider taping the students doing their "broadcast" so they can see for themselves how they did.

Activity 17
That's What They'd Say!

As a class, find two characters from a television show that the students all know. Select a video clip and have them make up dialog describing a selected scene from the character's point of view. Then, working in small groups, the students should choose two characters from a different television show they all know. Have them write dialog for the two characters using a selected clip. Allow the groups to read their dialog aloud -- in the voices of their characters if possible.

Activity 18
What's Next?

Select a clip from any bank and watch it as a class. Have the students brainstorm possibilities for what might happen in the next scene (or what might have happened in the previous scene). Then, working in small groups, have them write a two-paragraph narrative. The first paragraph should describe the scene from the video clip, and the second paragraph should describe what the students imagine happens in the next scene.

For example, here are two paragraphs using this idea based upon Clip #1 from the **Ocean's Island** bank:

We flew rapidly over the deep, blue ocean without any notion of where we were headed. All the officials from the Special Services Unit told us was that our help was needed right away. After a few minutes, we saw the waves crashing on the beach of the island in the distance, and knew we would be landing soon.

A car was waiting for us when we landed on the island. We were whisked away to meet with the Chief to find out how we could help. When we arrived at headquarters, she met us at the door and took us through the security checkpoint. Once we were seated in her office, she explained the mysterious disappearance of several important and valuable art objects. Our specialty is tracking down stolen items, so our purpose for being on the island was now clear.

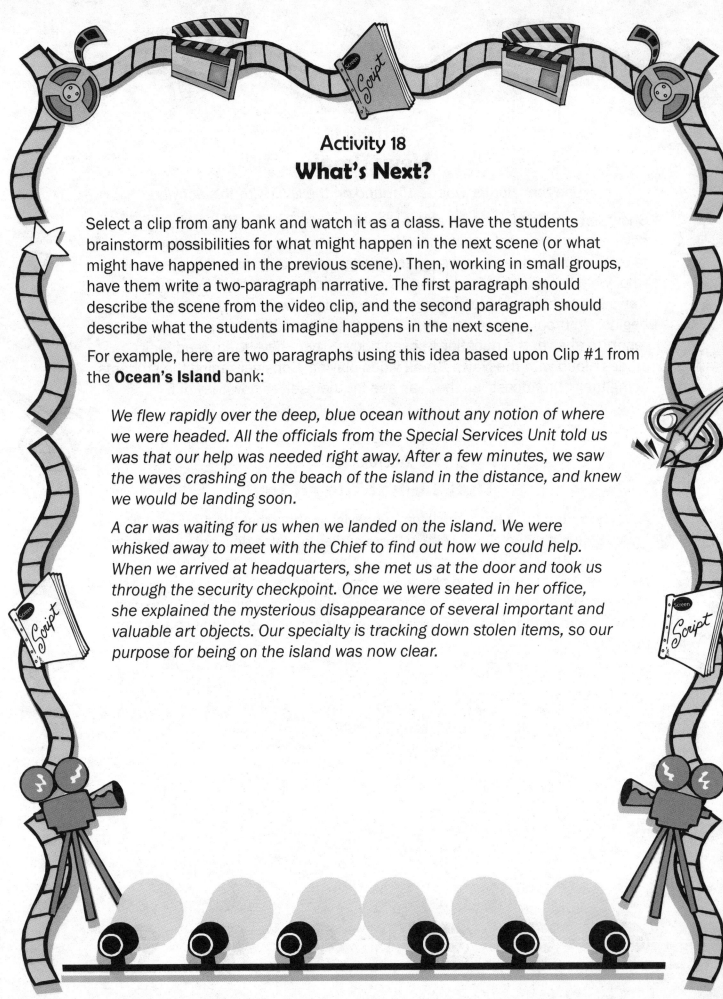

Activity 19
Select a Genre

As a class, or in small groups, view a selected clip from any of the banks. Discuss the various genres of movies listed below (refer to books the students might have read in similar genres) and decide the best category for the particular clip. Once a decision has been made, have the students write a paragraph describing the process they went through to decide on that genre. Next, have them write a paragraph on why a *different* genre might also be appropriate.

1. Western
2. Documentary
3. Comedy
4. Romance
5. Action/Adventure
6. Drama
7. Family
8. Sports
9. Mystery
10. Science Fiction
11. War
12. Horror
13. Biography

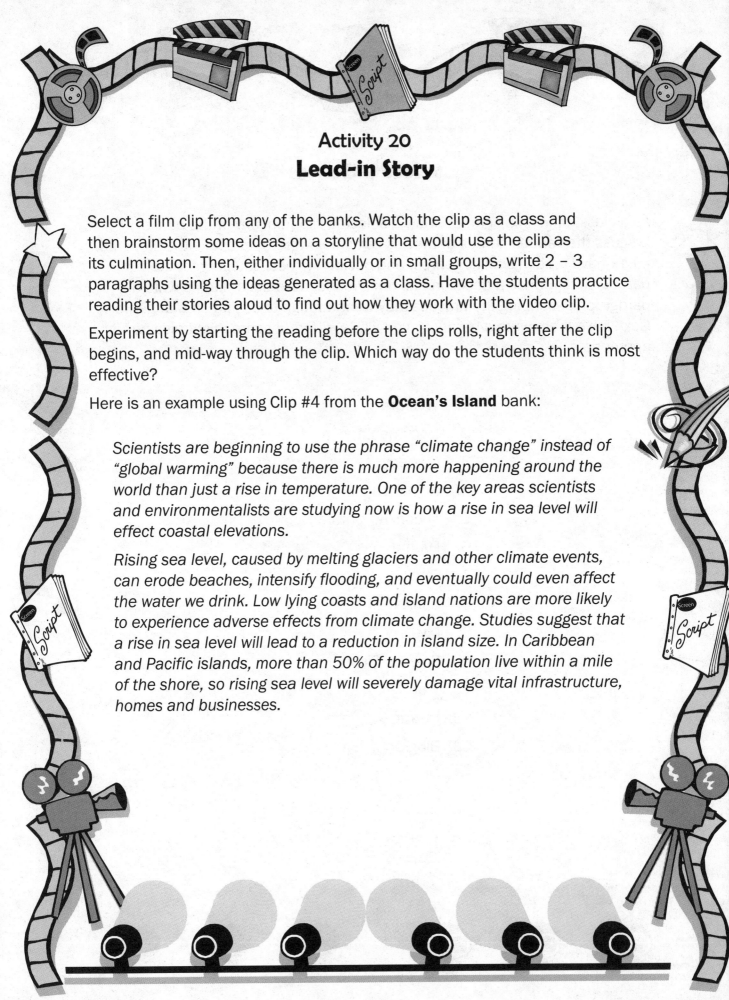

Activity 20
Lead-in Story

Select a film clip from any of the banks. Watch the clip as a class and then brainstorm some ideas on a storyline that would use the clip as its culmination. Then, either individually or in small groups, write 2 – 3 paragraphs using the ideas generated as a class. Have the students practice reading their stories aloud to find out how they work with the video clip.

Experiment by starting the reading before the clips rolls, right after the clip begins, and mid-way through the clip. Which way do the students think is most effective?

Here is an example using Clip #4 from the **Ocean's Island** bank:

Scientists are beginning to use the phrase "climate change" instead of "global warming" because there is much more happening around the world than just a rise in temperature. One of the key areas scientists and environmentalists are studying now is how a rise in sea level will effect coastal elevations.

Rising sea level, caused by melting glaciers and other climate events, can erode beaches, intensify flooding, and eventually could even affect the water we drink. Low lying coasts and island nations are more likely to experience adverse effects from climate change. Studies suggest that a rise in sea level will lead to a reduction in island size. In Caribbean and Pacific islands, more than 50% of the population live within a mile of the shore, so rising sea level will severely damage vital infrastructure, homes and businesses.

Activity 21
Famous First Lines

Pass out the "Famous First Lines" worksheet on page 22 to each student or each group of students. Not each of the "first lines" will necessarily have an appropriate film clip to go with it, but it is an engaging activity to try and find good matches whenever possible.

Have your students write several "first sentences" that they think would be good ways to begin a novel of their own.

Answers to worksheet:

1. <u>Harry Potter and the Sorcerer's Stone</u>, J.K. Rowling
2. <u>Peter Pan</u>, J.M. Barrie
3. <u>A Christmas Carol</u>, Charles Dickens
4. <u>The Hobbit</u>, J.R.R. Tolkien
5. <u>Charlie and the Chocolate Factory</u>, Roald Dahl
6. <u>To Kill A Mockingbird</u>, Harper Lee
7. <u>Robinson Crusoe</u>, Daniel Defoe

Activity 22
Mood Descriptors

Pass out the "Mood Descriptors" worksheet on page 23 and watch any clip. Have the students mark at least two mood descriptors that they feel are appropriate for the selected clip. Repeat this several times using the different lists on the worksheet. When this is completed, have the students identify other mood descriptors and write them on the bottom of the worksheet. This page will be a valuable reference for them in their own writing.

Activity 23
Topic Sentences #1

Use Clip #4 in the **From the Treetops** bank, Clip #2 in the **March of the Penguins** bank and Clip #4 in the **Tales of the Tribesmen** bank for this activity. Reproduce the worksheet on page 24 and give a copy to each student. After each clip, ask the students which sentence they choose, and why they think it is the best topic sentence.

After completing all three, play three different clips and have your students write their own topic sentences for each one.

Famous First Lines

Identify the authors of these famous "first lines" and the titles of the books from where they come. Then select a clip that you think works the best with one of the opening lines.

1. *Mr. and Mrs. Dursley, of number four, Privet Drive, were proud to say that they were perfectly normal, thank you very much.*

   Book Title:_____   Author: _____

2. *All children grow up, except one.*

   Book Title:_____   Author: _____

3. *Marley was dead, to begin with. There is no doubt whatever about that.*

   Book Title:_____   Author: _____

4. *In a hole in the ground there lived a hobbit.*

   Book Title:_____   Author _____

5. *These two very old people are the father and mother of Mr. Bucket.*

   Book Title:_____   Author: _____

6. *When he was nearly thirteen, my brother Jem got his arm badly broken at the elbow.*

   Book Title: _____   Author: _____

7. *I was born in the year 1632, in the city of York, of a good family, though not of that country, my father being a foreigner of Bremen, who settled first at Hull. He got a good estate by merchandise, and leaving off his trade lived afterward at York, from whence he had married my mother, whose relations were named Robinson, a good family in that country, and from whom I was called Robinson Kreutznear; but by the usual corruption of words in England we are now called, nay, we call ourselves, and write our name, Crusoe, and so my companions always called me.*

   Book Title:_____   Author: _____

Mood Descriptors

Mark two or more mood descriptors that you think are appropriate for each film clip.

Clip #1	Clip #2
_____ horrified	_____ energetic
_____ cheerful	_____ frantic
_____ tense	_____ excellent
_____ annoyed	_____ unhappy
_____ alert	_____ serious
_____ enthusiastic	_____ serene
_____ comfortable	_____ warm
_____ pleased	_____ sleepy
Clip #3	**Clip #4**
_____ worried	_____ reflective
_____ desolate	_____ sensational
_____ tense	_____ scared
_____ delighted	_____ calm
_____ outraged	_____ angry
_____ pleased	_____ relaxed
_____ restless	_____ cheerful
_____ content	_____ carefree
Clip #5	**Clip #6**
_____ excited	_____ carefree
_____ threatened	_____ tense
_____ distressed	_____ triumphant
_____ exuberant	_____ scared
_____ pleased	_____ festive
_____ annoyed	_____ serene
_____ delighted	_____ outraged
_____ happy	_____ energetic
_____ depressed	_____ anxious
_____ jealous	_____ cheerful

Topic Sentences

Every paragraph needs a topic sentence. Remember - a topic sentence is usually the first sentence of any paragraph. It is what we call the "topic" or what you're talking about in your writing!

**After you watch the first film clip, evaluate these topic sentences
and select the one you think is the best.**

1. Monkeys are animals.

2. Monkeys are playful, acrobatic animals.

3. Dead trees are a good place to find monkeys.

4. Circus music sounds funny.

**After you watch the second film clip, evaluate these topic sentences
and select the one you think is best.**

1. Penguins are among the most social of all birds, and often travel, swim, and feed in groups.

2. Almost all penguins are black and white.

3. Most scientists recognize 17 species of penguins.

4. The first penguin fossil fragments were found in New Zealand.

**After you watch the third film clip, evaluate these topic sentences
and select the one you think is best.**

1. Lions live in Africa.

2. Lions only spend four to five hours a day on the prowl, which means they sleep up to twenty hours a day.

3. The female lion is the primary hunter.

4. Many types of trees are found in Africa.

SECTION 3:
One to Two Lesson Activities

(Based on a 45 – 50 minute class period)

Activity 24
Which Works?

Compare and contrast using a Venn diagram

As a class, watch Clip #1 from the **Ancient Egypt** bank. Ask the students to give you some descriptive words and phrases that come to mind as they watch this clip and write them on the board. Then watch each of the next three versions of the clip, pausing after each to create a new list of descriptive words. After viewing all four clips, you should have something like this:

Clip #1 (no music)	Clip #2	Clip #3	Clip #4
lonely	reflective	tense	energetic
serene	serene	panic	action
sad	peaceful	scared	loud
scared	calm	threatened	frantic
calm	slow	action	quick

Finally, discuss which of the music clips makes the most sense with the scene. Demonstrate how to use a Venn diagram to organize the similarities and differences between their selections. A worksheet your students can use is on page 27. Then, have them write a three paragraph 'compare and contrast' essay using the choice they feel is the best vs. one of the other clips from the same bank.

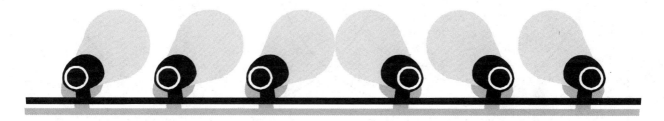

Use the example below to demonstrate how to use a Venn diagram to help organize the similarities and differences between their selections. In this example, Clip #1 and Clip #2 are comparable and Clip #3 is in contrast to Clip #1.

Film Clip #1	Film Clip #2	Film Clip #3
lonely	serene	tense
sad	peaceful	panic
serene	calm	scared
scared	content	threatened
calm	slow	action

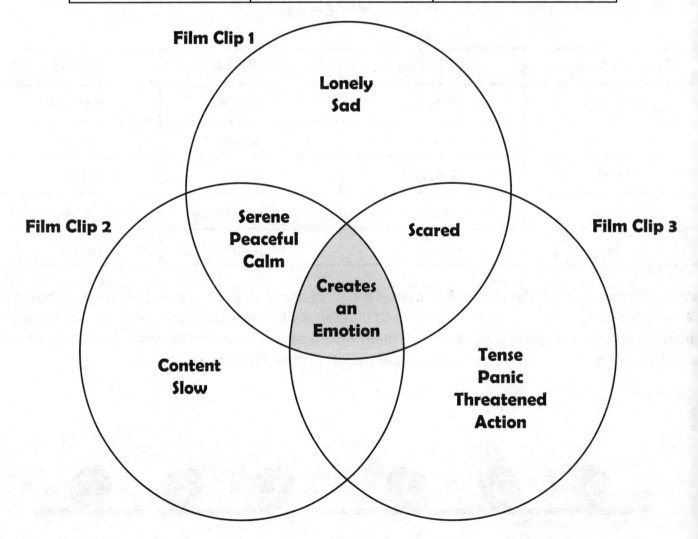

Name _____   Date_____

Which Works?

Compare and contrast using a Venn diagram

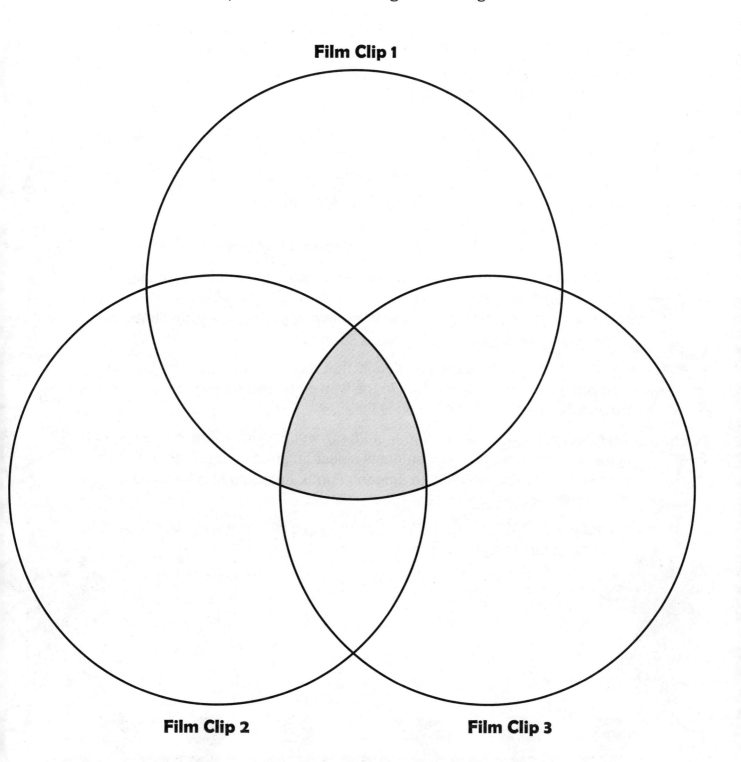

Film Clip 1

Film Clip 2

Film Clip 3

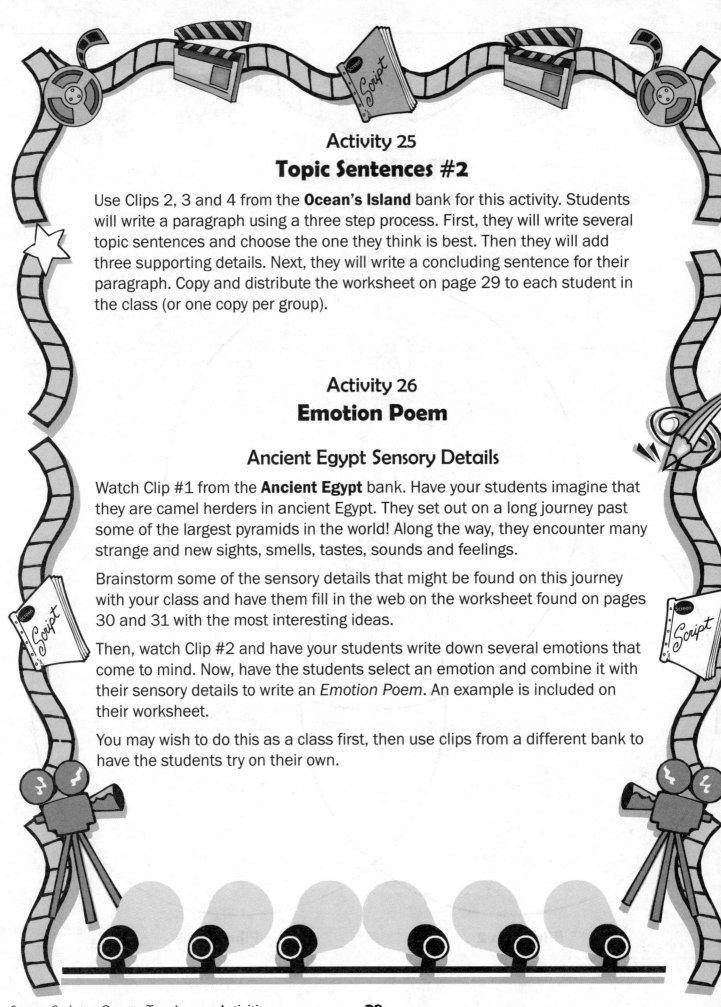

Activity 25
Topic Sentences #2

Use Clips 2, 3 and 4 from the **Ocean's Island** bank for this activity. Students will write a paragraph using a three step process. First, they will write several topic sentences and choose the one they think is best. Then they will add three supporting details. Next, they will write a concluding sentence for their paragraph. Copy and distribute the worksheet on page 29 to each student in the class (or one copy per group).

Activity 26
Emotion Poem

Ancient Egypt Sensory Details

Watch Clip #1 from the **Ancient Egypt** bank. Have your students imagine that they are camel herders in ancient Egypt. They set out on a long journey past some of the largest pyramids in the world! Along the way, they encounter many strange and new sights, smells, tastes, sounds and feelings.

Brainstorm some of the sensory details that might be found on this journey with your class and have them fill in the web on the worksheet found on pages 30 and 31 with the most interesting ideas.

Then, watch Clip #2 and have your students write down several emotions that come to mind. Now, have the students select an emotion and combine it with their sensory details to write an *Emotion Poem*. An example is included on their worksheet.

You may wish to do this as a class first, then use clips from a different bank to have the students try on their own.

A Good Topic Sentence Works Wonders!

rite a different topic sentence for each of the three film clips you see.

_____

_____

_____

elect one of your topic sentences and add three supporting details.

nese supporting details should relate to the topic sentence that you chose.

_____

_____

_____

concluding sentence concludes or ends your paragraph. It wraps everything up and ties it together, most like a summary.

rite a concluding sentence for your paragraph. _____

_____

Sample paragraph:

Topic sentence: The ocean and its mysteries have fascinated people for centuries.

Supporting Details:

1. Around the year 900, the Vikings begin to explore and colonize Iceland, Greenland, and Newfoundland. They were among the first to use the North Star to determine their latitude.

2. In 1807, President Thomas Jefferson created an agency called "United States Coast Survey." This agency began the formal study of the gulf stream.

3. In 1999, an ocean explorer named Robert Ballard began combing the floor of the Black Sea in search of the remains of ancient dwellings which might provide insights into the story of Noah and the Arc.

Concluding Sentence: Almost 95 per cent of the ocean has not been studied yet, so its mysteries will probably continue to fascinate people for centuries to come.

Emotion Poem
Ancient Egypt Sensory Details

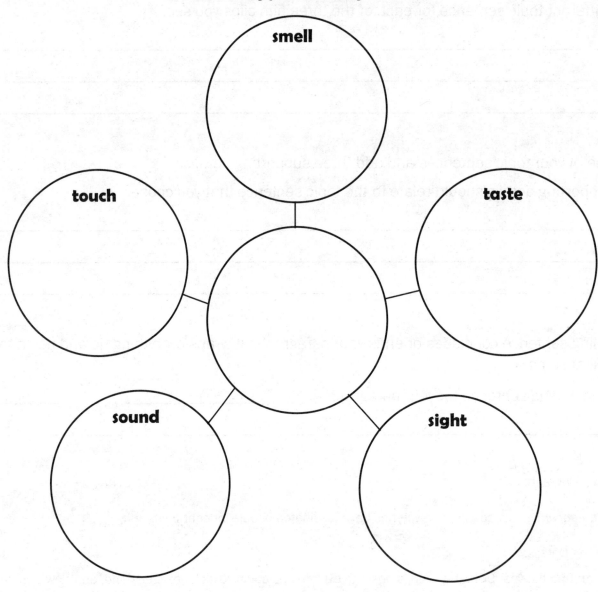

After you watch Clip #2, write down some emotions that come to mind.

1. _____

2. _____

3. _____

ow it's time to write an *Emotion Poem*. Select one of the emotions you wrote down for the clip and ombine it with the sensory details from the web you created.

ere is an example...

Anger

nger is a pyramid made of stone

nger is the smell of nothingness from the wind

nger is the taste of sand in your mouth

nger is the feel of the desert sun pounding on your back

nger is the sound of sand flailing past your ears

tle (the emotion chosen): _____

ne 1 (sight)_____ is _____

ne 2 (smell_____ is _____

ne 3 (taste) _____ is _____

ne 4 (touch/feel) _____ is _____

ne 5 (sound) _____ is _____

peat the activity individually or in small groups using two clips from a different bank.

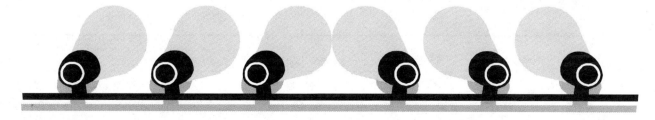

Sensory Details (from Clip #1)

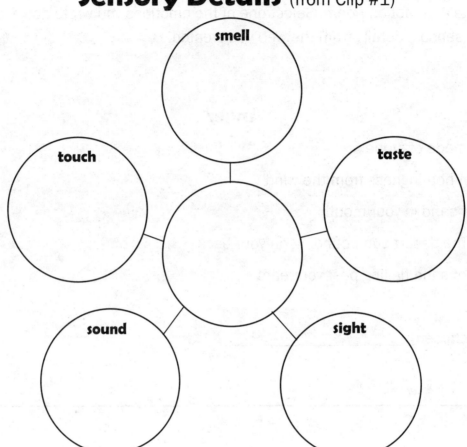

smell

touch

taste

sound

sight

Emotions (from Clip #2)

1. _____

2. _____

3. _____

Title (emotion): _____

Line 1 (sight) _____ is _____

Line 2 (smell) _____ _____

Line 3 (taste) _____ is _____

Line 4 (touch) _____ is _____

Line 5 (sound) _____ is _____

Activity 27
Now Sell It!

*Use the videos in the **Now Sell It** menu for this activity*

nce students are familiar with persuasive speeches, introduce various concepts that are used in television, radio, print and internet advertising to convince people to buy a product or service. Some amples of advertising types include:

- Promise a benefit
- Mention a problem
- Inject drama
- Make it human
- New and improved
- That's news
- Differentiate
- Save at the sale
- Make a metaphor
- "How to"
- Simplify
- Brand character
- Attack
- Offer extras
- Trigger emotion
- Enter to win
- What's the story?

ther individually or in small groups, have students select one of the five videos from Bonus Menu 2 on e DVD (**Now Sell It**) and create the dialog for a television advertisement that sells the product. If time ermits, have students design posters and packaging for their product.

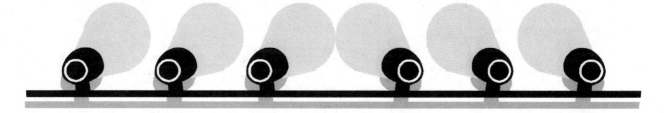

Activity 28
Treasure Hunt

Use Clips 2, 3 or 4 from the **Do You Like to Fly?** bank. Have the students imagine that the passengers on the plane are treasure hunters, then have them write a paragraph that answers the "who, what, where, when, why and how" questions about the treasure hunters and the treasure. For example:

Sophie, Denzel and Ray had been friends all through high school and college. They never realized that their friendship would bring them together on an adventure like this though! While doing research three months ago on some old land titles, Ray discovered a map that looked like it showed the location of the long lost money from the 1963 Great Train Robbery in England. He called his friend Sophie, who is a cartographer, and she called Denzel, who is a pilot. The three have been planning this trip to central Mexico to follow the details of the map ever since.

Give your students the organizer on page 35 to help them get started.

Activity 29
Who, What, When, Where, Why, How #2

Use Clips 2, 3 or 4 from the **Mad Rush** bank in this second "who, what, where, when, why and how" activity. Have your students (individually or in groups) select one of the people from the crowd. Have the students focus on their facial expressions and body language to create a composite of this person.

Who are they? What were they doing before they began walking down the sidewalk? Where are they going now? What time do they have to be there? Why are they going there? Will they walk the whole way there?

If you wish, give your students the organizer on page 36 to help them get started.

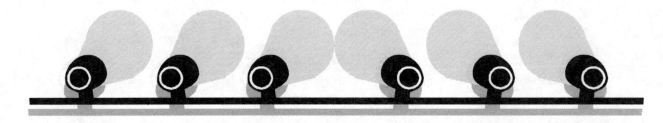

Treasure Hunt Web

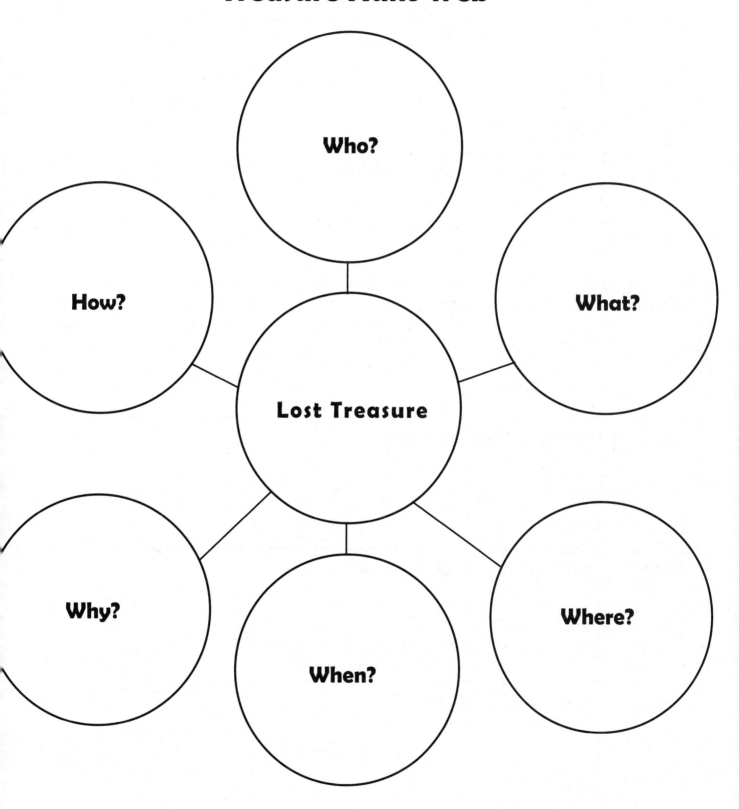

Who?

How?

What?

Lost Treasure

Why?

When?

Where?

W5H Organizer

Who	Description/name of person:
What	What were they doing before?
Where	Where are they going now?
Why	Why are they going there?
When	When do they need to arrive?
How	How will they get there?

Activity 30
Story Starters

ssign (or have students select) one of the film clips listed below, along with one of the "story starters" ted. Depending on the age and skills of your class, have them write 1 – 3 paragraphs using their osen story starter.

ght Vision, Clip #3

1. I never thought I could do it, but...

2. I knew it was going to be an unusual day when my mom woke me up and told me to get in the helicopter.

3. Flying over the city, we knew we might already be too late.

You Like to Fly?, Clip #4

1. I watched in horror as we flew over the rough terrain.

2. The moment I had been dreading for weeks was finally here.

3. We were the only people who knew the truth about...

isode in Space, Clip #2

1. I knew that if I didn't get nervous, I would be able to...

2. I shouted into the radio: "Get out of there as fast as you can!"

3. Everyone knew that there was going to be an explosion, but nobody knew that...

ad Rush, Clip #3

1. Even though the sidewalk was jammed with people, I knew we were going to have a great day.

2. Somehow, I managed to get lost again, but I had a feeling it would turn into a fun adventure.

3. Today is the day! I am finally going to...

Activity 31
Connections

Note: This activity uses the 5 bonus tracks on the DVD in the "Bonus Videos 3" menu

Have students choose one of the selections from the Bonus Videos 3 on the DVD, then have them writ
a 2 - 3 paragraph persuasive speech that begins:

1. "If we don't do something about _____" or...

2. "Concerned citizens need to be more aware of_____" or...

3. "What the world needs now is_____" or...

4. "Extreme sports can be _____" or...

5. "Safety is a prime consideration when _____" or...

6. "Television is _____" or...

7. "Aliens are able to _____" or...

8. "The trouble with _____ is" or...

9. One of your (or their) own choosing.

Activity 32
Screen Scripts #1

Note: This activity uses the 5 bonus tracks on the DVD in the "Bonus Videos 3" menu.

his activity focuses on writing a movie script or "screenplay." Vocabulary words and phrases as they
late to writing a screenplay include:

1. *concept:* a one or two sentence summary of the screenplay

2. *the pitch:* describing the screenplay by relating it to other movies..."it's like Harry Potter combined with Spiderman..."

3. *launch pad:* a place to get ideas for a screenplay; another movie, a book, a newspaper article, a television or web advertisement, etc. In this case, the dialog for the script will be written based on which of the five videos is selected.

4. *synopsis:* the general outline of the story with a beginning, middle and end.

5. *primary slug*: a heading with three pieces of information...interior (INT.) / exterior (EXT.), place, and time of day. For example:

     INT. Captain Van der Meer's Castle – Evening

6. *secondary slug:* a heading with more detail. For example:

                                   CUT TO:
                          SUIT OF ARMOR IN CORNER
                          eyes are visible inside the helmet

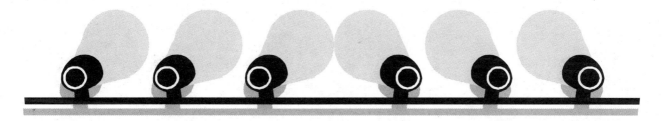

The goal of this activity is to learn how to develop characters and create dialog using the videos provided in the "Bonus Videos 3" menu.

Here is a sample script using the **Mad City** video:

_____

EXT. Busy New York street – Night *(primary slug)*

There is action on the street. It is so crowded with people and vehicles that traffic is at a standstill. *(briefly describe the scene)*

UNSEEN CHARACTER STUCK IN TRAFFIC
(angry)
This is the third time today that I have
wasted time stuck in traffic. It is
really starting to annoy me.

COMPANION IN CAR
(jovial)
Yes, but don't you love the feeling of
excitement in the air?
People are happy to be with
their friends in the city. There
is so much to do, and so much to
see...theatre, music, restaurants,
movies, museums...

PERSON 1
(cuts off person 2 in mid-sentence)
Not really. In the time I've been here
all I've dreamed about is the beautiful,
peaceful places where I grew up.

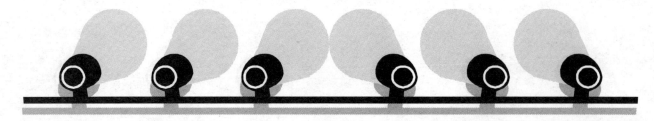

CUT TO:

EXT. RIVER FLY OVER - MID-AFTERNOON (primary slug)
We had sparkling rivers and wide
open spaces. The forest was thick
and lush. We could while away the
hours rowing around the river in
our small boat fishing, or just
doing nothing.

PERSON 2
But what did you do for fun?

PERSON 1
Trust me, we had plenty of adventures
exploring the river banks. There was always
something new and different to see.

CUT TO:

EXT. BADLANDS FLY OVER – DAY *(primary slug)*

(wistfully)
And, we always spent two weeks in the spring
with our grandparents in Arizona. They had a
huge ranch where we could roam
free each day.

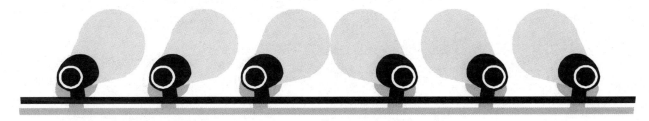

Activity 33
It's Greek to Me

"It's Greek to Me" is a zany way to highlight the power of facial and body expressions along with tone of voice. Have the students select a clip on their own and write a short, but *emotional* persuasive speech. They will then give their speech to the class, but they have to use a "made-up" language. Anything will work – the point is to try to convey their message to the listeners using facial and body expressions along with tone of voice. It takes practice, but this activity is lots of fun and will really help students break out of the "stand and speak" rut.

Activity 34
TV Teaser

There are several options for this activity. The main idea is to write a descriptive paragraph to go along with a selected film clip that is a promotional spot for a television show. Some of the options include:

1. Giving students the name of the show they are writing about (<u>America's Most Wanted</u> using Clip #4 from **Mad Rush**, for example)

2. Giving students the channel that their show is on (The History Channel using Clip #2 from **Ancient Egypt**, for example)

Another option is for you to write the introduction and relate it to something that your class is studying. As an example, if your students are familiar with the U.S. Constitution and the Bill of Rights, it might be interesting for you to do something along these lines using Clip #4 from **Mad Rush**:

Tonight on <u>America's Most Wanted</u>, police will search the crowded streets of New York City looking for a criminal who has eluded them for years. The police won't be on the streets with a photograph of the suspect though...instead, officers at a central location will use facial scanning software to identify the criminal by scanning the faces of everyone on this busy New York street.

You could then discuss with your students the implications of this technology and whether or not its use violates individual's civil rights. You might also branch out into possible applications for software in the future or how technology has affected our society.

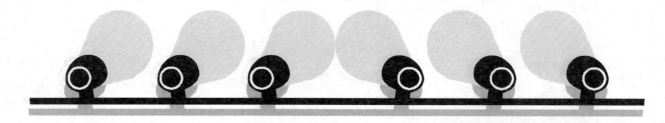

Activity 35
Research: Ancient Egypt

esearch the history of ancient Egypt using a combination of written materials and websites including:

1. www.historyforkids.org (navigate to Egypt)

2. www.ancient-egypt.org

3. www.ancientegypt.co.uk

udy the following information and then have students write a narrative essay.

inciples of writing a narrative essay

1. Involve readers in the story

2. Be sure there is a generalization in your essay that will take on meaning for your readers

3. The main component of a narrative is the story, so details must be selected to support, explain and enhance the story.

nventions of narrative essays

1. Usually written in the first person (I) or the third person (he, she)

2. Concrete sensory details are used to create a memorable impression, for example, the sentence "It was windy" becomes more vivid for the reader if is expanded like this: "The sandy grit carried by the unrelenting wind chaffed the skin on my face and neck."

3. Spatial-Order relationships can add descriptive details, too. For example, "The Bent Pyramid by Snofru sits in the heart of Dashur." is better than "The Bent Pyramid is in Dashur."

4. Narratives should include a plot (including setting and characters), a climax and an ending.

e software <u>Storybook Weaver</u>, published by The Learning Company, is a helpful tool for students aged – 12. It is available at Amazon, Barnes and Noble, Borders, and many other booksellers.

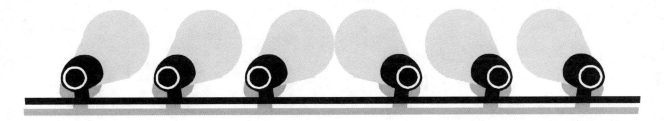

Activity 36
Screen Soundtrack

Consider the function of a movie soundtrack. What is its purpose? It is supposed to enhance whatever is going on in the scene, but must fit with the mood, or feelings of the characters in the movie. How do the producers, writers and directors choose the proper music to go with each scene? Let's find out!

The purpose of the activity/project is to combine your love of music and lyrics, creative talent, and interpretation of each movie clip. This project has three parts: the selection of the songs, a written essay, and presentation for your classmates.

Step one: As you rewatch each movie clip (without any music), select three for which you feel you can interpret the theme or mood. In other words, what is the main feeling or impression that you feel after watching the clip? Does it make you feel happy? angry? excited? If people were in these scenes, what they would be thinking or doing? Choose songs (these can be any songs... especially current ones!) that you think fit with the mood of the movie clip. Copy or print the lyrics from the internet, or type them out. (please make sure all song lyrics are school appropriate).

Step Two: Once you have finished selecting the songs for three of the movie clips, compose an essay explaining why you selected each song and how the song represents the mood, or feeling of the movie clip. You should have an introductory paragraph, three body paragraphs (one for each song selection) and a conclusion paragraph.

Step Three: For the day the project is due, prepare a three minute presentation including a CD from one of the songs you chose. Play that song for the class and discuss why you chose it and what the lyrics mean to you in context with the movie clip.

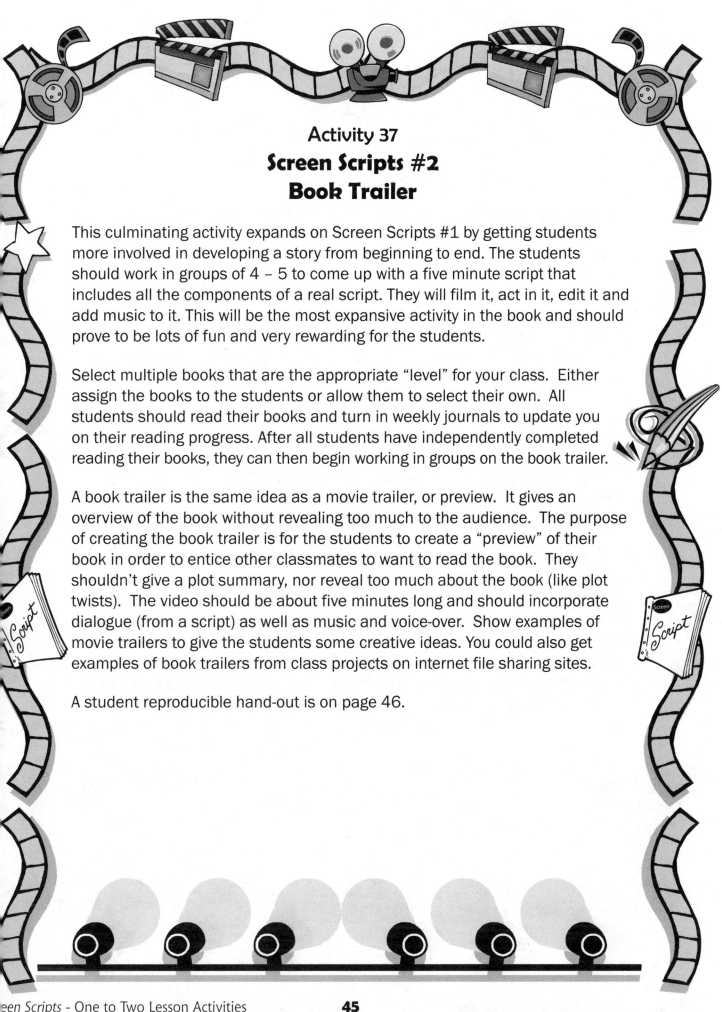

Activity 37
Screen Scripts #2
Book Trailer

This culminating activity expands on Screen Scripts #1 by getting students more involved in developing a story from beginning to end. The students should work in groups of 4 – 5 to come up with a five minute script that includes all the components of a real script. They will film it, act in it, edit it and add music to it. This will be the most expansive activity in the book and should prove to be lots of fun and very rewarding for the students.

Select multiple books that are the appropriate "level" for your class. Either assign the books to the students or allow them to select their own. All students should read their books and turn in weekly journals to update you on their reading progress. After all students have independently completed reading their books, they can then begin working in groups on the book trailer.

A book trailer is the same idea as a movie trailer, or preview. It gives an overview of the book without revealing too much to the audience. The purpose of creating the book trailer is for the students to create a "preview" of their book in order to entice other classmates to want to read the book. They shouldn't give a plot summary, nor reveal too much about the book (like plot twists). The video should be about five minutes long and should incorporate dialogue (from a script) as well as music and voice-over. Show examples of movie trailers to give the students some creative ideas. You could also get examples of book trailers from class projects on internet file sharing sites.

A student reproducible hand-out is on page 46.

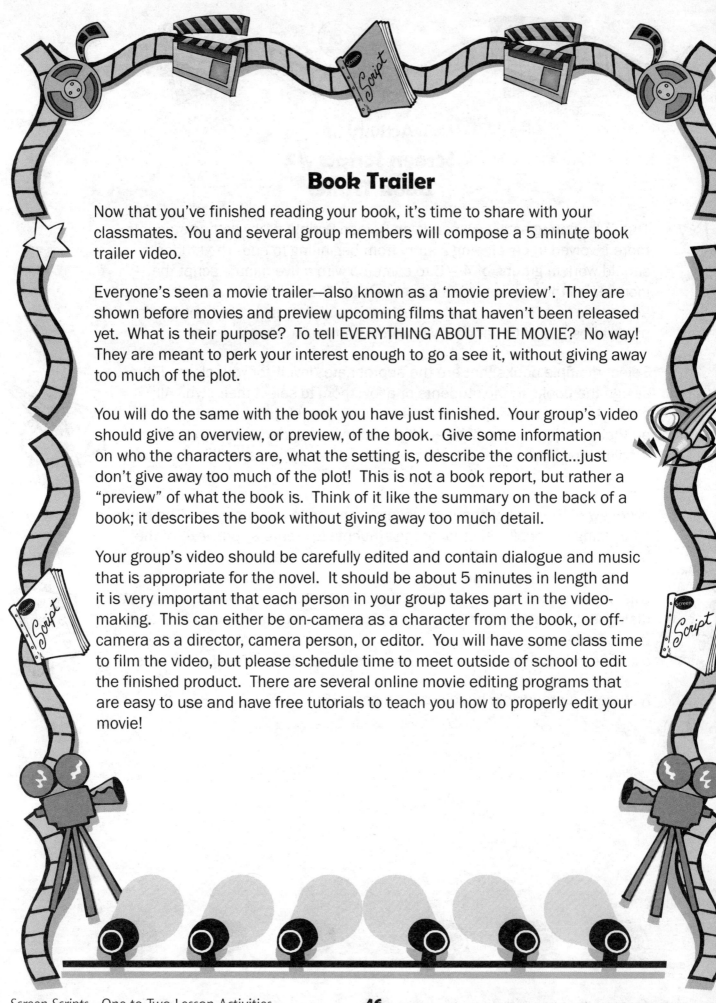

Book Trailer

Now that you've finished reading your book, it's time to share with your classmates. You and several group members will compose a 5 minute book trailer video.

Everyone's seen a movie trailer—also known as a 'movie preview'. They are shown before movies and preview upcoming films that haven't been released yet. What is their purpose? To tell EVERYTHING ABOUT THE MOVIE? No way! They are meant to perk your interest enough to go a see it, without giving away too much of the plot.

You will do the same with the book you have just finished. Your group's video should give an overview, or preview, of the book. Give some information on who the characters are, what the setting is, describe the conflict...just don't give away too much of the plot! This is not a book report, but rather a "preview" of what the book is. Think of it like the summary on the back of a book; it describes the book without giving away too much detail.

Your group's video should be carefully edited and contain dialogue and music that is appropriate for the novel. It should be about 5 minutes in length and it is very important that each person in your group takes part in the video-making. This can either be on-camera as a character from the book, or off-camera as a director, camera person, or editor. You will have some class time to film the video, but please schedule time to meet outside of school to edit the finished product. There are several online movie editing programs that are easy to use and have free tutorials to teach you how to properly edit your movie!

Film Editing Terms:

t

A visual transition created in editing in which one shot is instantaneously replaced on screen by another.

ntinuity editing

Editing that creates action that flows smoothly across shots and scenes without jarring visual inconsistencies; establishes a sense of story for the viewer.

ss cutting

Cutting back and forth quickly between two or more lines of action, indicating they are happening simultaneously.

lve

A gradual scene transition. The editor overlaps the end of one shot with the beginning of the next one.

iting

The work of selecting and joining together shots to create a finished film.

rors of continuity

Disruptions in the flow of a scene, such as a failure to match action or the placement of props across shots.

tablishing shot

A shot, normally taken from a great distance or from a "bird's eye view," that establishes where the action is about to occur.

eline match

The matching of eyelines between two or more characters. For example, if Sam looks to the right in shot A, Jean will look to the left in shot B. This establishes a relationship of proximity and continuity.

de

A visual transition between shots or scenes that appears on screen as a brief interval with no picture. The editor fades one shot to black and then fades in the next. Often used to indicate a change in time and place.

al cut

The finished edit of a film, approved by the director and the producer. This is what the audience sees.

jump cut

A cut that creates a lack of continuity by leaving out parts of the action.

matched cut

A cut joining two shots whose compositional elements match, helping to establish strong continuity action.

montage

Scenes whose emotional impact and visual design are achieved through the editing together of man brief shots. The shower scene from *Psycho* is an example of montage editing.

rough cut

The editor's first pass at assembling the shots into a film, before tightening and polishing occurs.

sequence shot

A long take that extends for an entire scene or sequence. It is composed of only one shot with no editing.

shot reverse shot cutting

Usually used for conversation scenes, this technique alternates between over-the-shoulder shots showing each character speaking.

Courtesy of Annenberg Media

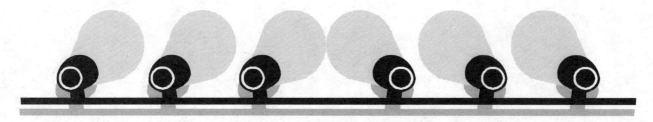